EYE TO EYE
with Cats

SIAMESE CATS

Lynn M. Stone

ROURKE PUBLISHING
Vero Beach, Florida 32964

www.rourkepublishing.com

PHOTO CREDITS: Page 9: © Anja Hild; All other photos © Lynn M. Stone.

Editor: Jeanne Sturm

Cover and page design by Heather Botto

Library of Congress Cataloging-in-Publication Data

Printed in the USA

Library of Congress Cataloging-in-Publication Data

Stone, Lynn M.
 Siamese cats / Lynn M. Stone.
     p. cm. -- (Eye to eye with cats)
 Includes index.
 ISBN 978-1-60694-335-9 (hard cover)
 ISBN 978-1-60694-861-3 (soft cover)
 1. Siamese cat--Juvenile literature. I. Title.
 SF449.S5S762 2010
 636.8'25--dc22
                                        2009005985

Printed in the USA

CG/CG

www.rourkepublishing.com - rourke@rourkepublishing.com
Post Office Box 643328 Vero Beach, Florida 32964

Table of Contents

Siamese Cats

The Siamese may be the best-known **breed**, or kind, of cat on planet Earth. Its unusual voice is a good match for its unusual looks and doglike behavior.

Siamese are famous for their loud voices, attention to their human families, and colored **points**.

Siamese cats are one of the four types of cats considered to be Oriental breeds.

The Siamese's Looks

A cat's points are its **extremities**: the face, paws, legs, tail, and ears. Siamese have dark points against lighter body fur.

While nearly all Siamese have blue eyes, short fur, and dark points, they can have strikingly different body types.

Siamese cats fall into four color categories: Seal Point, Chocolate Point, Blue Point, and Lilac Point.

The so-called modern Siamese is one of the greyhounds of the cat world. It is extremely long and slender with a wedge-shaped head, large ears, thin legs, and a whip-like tail.

The classic, or traditional, Siamese type has a much heavier body and more of an apple-shaped head. In 2007, The International Cat Association recognized the classic Siamese type as a separate breed, called the Thai cat.

Cat fanciers have used the Siamese as a base for at least a dozen new breeds of cats. One of these is the Oriental Shorthair. The Oriental Shorthair is a Siamese without colored points.

Oriental Shorthairs, with their elongated bodies, are one of the modern Siamese breeds. In 1977, the Cat Fancier's Association added them to the list of cats elegible for championship status.

Purebred Siamese

The Siamese is one of about 40 cat breeds recognized by the Cat **Fanciers** Association. Cats whose parents are both of the same breed are **purebreds**. A purebred Siamese kitten has two purebred Siamese parents.

Purebred kittens typically grow up with the same kind of fur and body shape as their parents. Traditional type Siamese parents, for example, produce kittens of the same type.

Some kittens are born without colored points. By the time a kitten is four weeks old, the fur on its points will have changed colors.

10

The great majority of cats are not purebreds. Cat fanciers like the fact that purebreds are **predictable**. They show certain qualities over and over again.

Siamese cats are social and intelligent.

A purebred Siamese kitten will most likely grow up to have the same qualities and faults as its parents.

The Cat for You?

A Siamese cat is like a fire on the stove; it cannot be ignored. While a Siamese cat may demand attention, it is a wonderfully active, **affectionate**, and chatty companion.

The doglike reputation of Siamese cats comes from their willingness to walk on a leash, play fetch, and enjoy human companionship.

If you choose a Siamese cat for your pet, be prepared to give it lots of attention. Siamese cats can be quite mischievous when they are lonely.

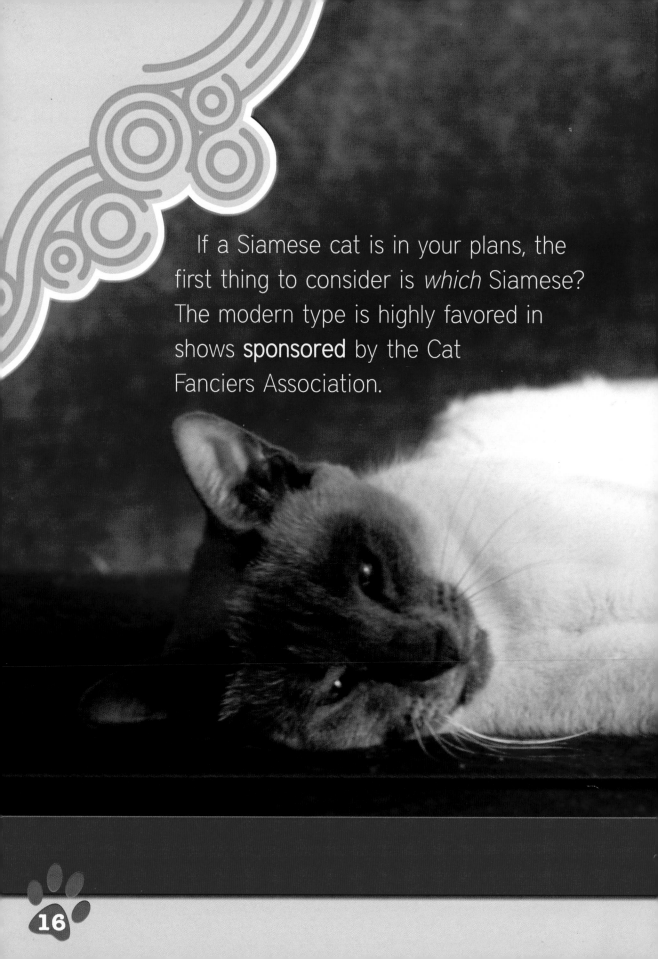

If a Siamese cat is in your plans, the first thing to consider is *which* Siamese? The modern type is highly favored in shows **sponsored** by the Cat Fanciers Association.

Not everyone, of course, favors the modern type. Fans in growing numbers prefer the more plump, classic style Siamese cat.

The Cat Fancier's Association sets standards for each cat breed. When judges award points to a Siamese cat, they look for many things, including a wedge-shaped head, almond-shaped eyes, and a cat in good physical condition.

The History of Siamese Cats

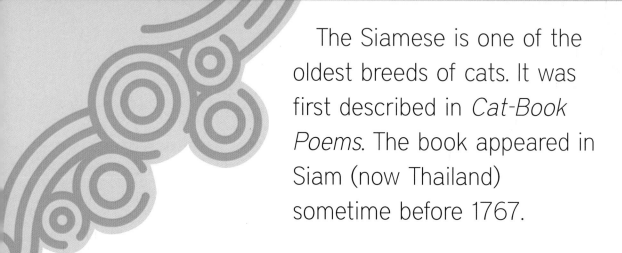

The Siamese is one of the oldest breeds of cats. It was first described in *Cat-Book Poems*. The book appeared in Siam (now Thailand) sometime before 1767.

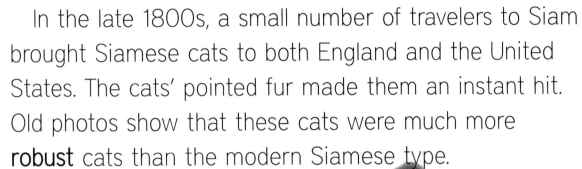

In the late 1800s, a small number of travelers to Siam brought Siamese cats to both England and the United States. The cats' pointed fur made them an instant hit. Old photos show that these cats were much more **robust** cats than the modern Siamese type.

Early Siamese cats had crossed eyes and kinked tails; traits that have disappeared through careful breeding.

Such films as *That Darn Cat, The Incredible Journey*, and *The Lady and the Tramp* helped make Siamese cats even more popular in the 1950s and 1960s. After the 1960s, fanciers began to favor the modern Siamese type.

Traditional Siamese, however, are making a comeback. In 2001, North American fanciers imported more of the traditional Siamese from Thailand to improve that breed line in the Western World.

ABOUT CAT BREEDS

The beginnings of domestic, or tame, cats date back at least 8,000 years, when people began to raise the kittens of small wild cats. By 4,000 years ago, the Egyptians had totally tame, household cats. Most actual breeds of cats, however, are fewer than 150 years old. People created breeds by selecting parent cats that had certain qualities people liked and wanted to repeat. Two longhaired parents, for example, were likely to produce longhaired kittens. By carefully choosing cat parents, cat fanciers have managed to create cats with predictable qualities — breeds.

Siamese Cat Facts

- 🐾 Date of Origin – before 1700s
- 🐾 Place of Origin – Thailand
- 🐾 Overall Size – medium
- 🐾 Weight – 6-12 pounds (2.5-5.5 kilograms)
- 🐾 Coat – short
- 🐾 **Grooming** – infrequent
- 🐾 Activity Level – very high
- 🐾 **Temperament** – very affectionate, energetic, outgoing; needs attention
- 🐾 Voice – very vocal

Glossary

affectionate (uh-FEK-shuh-nuht): loving

breed (BREED): a particular kind of domestic animal, such as a Siamese cat

extremities (ek-STREM-i-teez): the outermost point or end of something, such as hands and feet

fanciers (FAN-see-erz): those who raise and work to improve purebred cats

grooming (GROOM-ing): the act of brushing, combing, and cleaning

points (POINTS): an animal's ears, face, tail, legs, and paws

predictable (pre-DIKT-uh-bul): that which can be decided before it happens

purebreds (PYOOR-bredz): animals with ancestors of the same breed

robust (roh-BUHST): built powerfully with some bulk

sponsored (SPON-surd): to be supported and organized by someone or some group

temperament (TEM-pur-uh-muhnt): an animal's nature or personality

Index

Websites to Visit

kids.cfa.org

www.ticaeo.com

www.cfainc.org/breeds/profiles/siamese.html

About the Author

A former teacher and sports writer, Lynn Stone is a widely published children's book author and nature photographer. He has photographed animals on all seven continents. The National Science Teachers Association chose one of his books, *Box Turtles*, as an Outstanding Science Trade Book for 2008. Stone, who grew up in Connecticut, lives in northern Illinois with his wife, golden retriever, two cats, and abundant fishing tackle.